Oklahoma

By Susan Labella

Subject Consultant
Bob Springer
Past State Geographer
Oklahoma City, Oklahoma

Reading Consultant
Cecilia Minden-Cupp, PhD
Former Director of the Language and Literacy Program
Harvard Graduate School of Education
Cambridge, Massachusetts

Children's Press®
A Division of Scholastic Inc.
New York   Toronto   London   Auckland   Sydney
Mexico City   New Delhi   Hong Kong
Danbury, Connecticut

Designer: Herman Adler
Photo Researcher: Caroline Anderson
The photo on the cover shows the sun setting over an Oklahoma prairie.

Library of Congress Cataloging-in-Publication Data

Labella, Susan, 1948–
    Oklahoma / by Susan Labella.
        p. cm. — (Rookie read-about geography)
    Includes index.
    ISBN 13: 978-0-516-25468-5 (lib. bdg.)   978-0-531-16817-2 (pbk.)
    ISBN 10: 0-516-25468-5 (lib. bdg.)   0-531-16817-4 (pbk.)
    1. Oklahoma—Juvenile literature. 2. Oklahoma—Geography—Juvenile
    literature. I. Title. II. Series.
    F694.3.L33 2007
    976.6—dc22   2006004586

CHILDREN'S PRESS, and ROOKIE READ-ABOUT®, and associated
logos are trademarks and/or registered trademarks of Scholastic Library
Publishing. SCHOLASTIC and associated logos are trademarks and/or
registered trademarks of Scholastic Inc.
1 2 3 4 5 6 7 8 9 10 R 16 15 14 13 12 11 10 09 08 07

An Oklahoma oil well

Which state is known for its oil, rodeos, and Native American festivals?

It's Oklahoma!

Oklahoma is in the southern part of the United States.

Can you find Oklahoma on this map?

CANADA

WASHINGTON
OREGON
IDAHO
MONTANA
NORTH DAKOTA
MINNESOTA
WISCONSIN
MICHIGAN
NEW HAMPSHIRE
VERMONT
MAINE

WYOMING
SOUTH DAKOTA

NEVADA
UTAH
COLORADO
NEBRASKA
IOWA
ILLINOIS
INDIANA
OHIO
NEW YORK
MASSACHUSETTS
RHODE ISLAND
CONNECTICUT
NEW JERSEY
DELAWARE
MARYLAND
PENNSYLVANIA

CALIFORNIA
ARIZONA
NEW MEXICO
KANSAS
MISSOURI
KENTUCKY
WEST VIRGINIA
VIRGINIA
Washington, D.C.

OKLAHOMA
ARKANSAS
TENNESSEE
NORTH CAROLINA

TEXAS
MISSISSIPPI
ALABAMA
GEORGIA
SOUTH CAROLINA

LOUISIANA
FLORIDA

North
West   East
South

ALASKA
CANADA
MEXICO

HAWAII

5

Oklahoma's Salt Plains

The Salt Plains are in northern Oklahoma. Salt covers the muddy ground in this area.

Crystals grow below the ground here. People visit the Salt Plains to dig for crystals.

What else grows in Oklahoma? Oklahoma farmers raise cattle, wheat, peaches, and peanuts.

An Oklahoma cattle farm

A working oil well stands near Oklahoma's state capitol.

Oklahoma is also famous for its oil. This oil can be used for products such as gasoline.

There's even a working oil well in front of the state capitol in Oklahoma City!

Forests cover nearly
one-fourth of Oklahoma.
Oklahoma's state tree is
the redbud.

The state wildflower is
the Indian blanket.

Indian blanket

Oklahoma's Wichita Mountains

14

Oklahoma has four
mountain ranges.
These are the Arbuckle,
Ouachita, Ozark, and
Wichita mountains.

Oklahoma's Red River flows between Oklahoma and Texas. It is perfect for canoeing, kayaking, and rafting!

The Red River

A scissor-tailed flycatcher

Grassy plains stretch across Oklahoma and are home to jackrabbits, coyotes, and prairie dogs.

Oklahoma's state bird is the scissor-tailed flycatcher.

The Museum of the
Great Plains is in Lawton.
Visitors there discover what
life was like in Oklahoma
hundreds of years ago.
They study Native
American tools and learn
how early settlers lived.

Visitors to the Museum of the Great Plains can explore a log cabin.

A Native American performs a traditional dance in Anadarko.

More Native Americans
live in Oklahoma than any
other state.

Anadarko holds a special
festival each year to honor
Native Americans.

The capital of Oklahoma is Oklahoma City.

Oklahoma City features a zoo and several museums, including the Cowboy Hall of Fame.

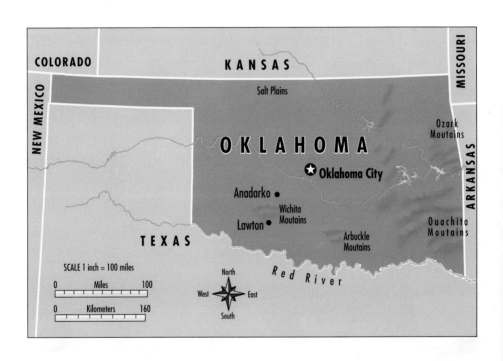

COLORADO

KANSAS

MISSOURI

NEW MEXICO

Salt Plains

OKLAHOMA

Ozark
Moutains

⭐ Oklahoma City

ARKANSAS

Anadarko ●

Wichita
Moutains

Lawton ●

Ouachita
Moutains

Arbuckle
Moutains

TEXAS

SCALE 1 inch = 100 miles

Red River

0   Miles   100

North

0   Kilometers   160

West ✴ East

South

25

An Oklahoma cowboy performs during a rodeo.

Oklahoma City also hosts a state fair.

Visitors to the state fair can watch a rodeo. This is a contest where cowboys and cowgirls try to ride wild horses and bulls.

There is so much to see
and do in Oklahoma!

What will you do first
when you get there?

Native American girls in traditional dress in Anadarko

Words You Know

cattle

Indian blanket

Red River

rodeo

30

Salt Plains

scissor-tailed flycatcher

state capitol

Wichita Mountains

Index

About the Author

Susan Labella is a former teacher and editor. She is currently a freelance writer and has written other books in the Rookie Read-About® Geography series.

Photo Credits

Photographs © 2007: AP/Wide World Photos/Ed Blochowiak/Shawnee News-Star: 26, 30 bottom right; Buddy Mays/Travel Stock: 13, 30 top right; Corbis Images: 3 (Lowell Georgia), 29 (Lindsay Hebberd), 10, 31 bottom left (Dave G. Houser/Post-Houserstock); John Elk III: 6, 21, 22, 31 top left; Photo Researchers, NY/Steve and Dave Maslowski: 18, 31 top right; Tom Bean: cover, 9, 14, 30 top left, 31 bottom right; Unicorn Stock Photos/Chuck Schmeiser: 17, 30 bottom left.

Maps by Bob Italiano